RUN, JUMP, AND THROW: HOW TO GET RECRUITED FOR COLLEGE TRACK & FIELD AND CROSS COUNTRY

VINCENT BINGHAM

Praise for *Run, Jump, and Throw: How to Get Recruited for College Track & Field and Cross Country*

"Coach Bingham's book will place many parents and athletes ahead of the recruiting process. Priceless!"

Coach Connie Teaberry

Olympian
Head Coach and Director of Track and Field and Cross Country,
Northern Illinois University, DeKalb, IL

"Coach Vince Bingham is one of my favorite and most trusted coaches at the college level."

Coach Joe Bill Dixon

Member, Missouri Sports Hall of Fame
25 State High School Team Championships,
West Plains High School, West Plains, MO

"Run, Jump and Throw is a great resource for any athlete wanting to compete in Track and Field at the collegiate level. It provides thorough explanations of every aspect of the recruiting process as well as a multitude of simple, yet great insights which will help prepare coaches, athletes and their families for one of the biggest decisions of their lives."

Coach Sean O'Connor

2015 Missouri High School Coach of the Year,
Lafayette High School, Wildwood, MO

"By understanding the concepts put forth in this book, students and coaches can have a better understanding of how to optimize the chances for a scholarship opportunity that will be the best situation for the athlete."

Coach Bryant Wright

2014, 2016 Missouri High School Coach of the Year
8 State High School Team Championships,
Festus High School, Festus, MO

"Am thankful for the process and will forever be grateful."

Nickeisha Anderson

Olympian
Jamaica

TABLE OF CONTENTS

www.CoachVinceBingham.com

INTRODUCTION

I grew up in a small town about 30 minutes south of St. Louis, Missouri, in a little town called Crystal City. I did not grow up in an affluent part of this small town. In fact, it was pretty much the opposite.

My mom worked hard at a local tavern, and my siblings and I played in the park and in the streets throughout the neighborhood after school while she was at work. I didn't pay much attention to my studies, and since Mom was working most of the time, I didn't have anyone around to make me pay attention.

If it weren't for track and field, I suspect my life would have turned out much differently. God blessed me with a peer group of great friends. I grew up with a guy named Jimmy Jennings, who to this day still holds a national Amateur Athletic Union (AAU) track and field record for the 1500 meter run that he set when he was a kid.

Jimmy was, and still is, a winner. He has always been down-to-earth and a really nice guy. Even when he was a kid, people liked him and liked being around him. I certainly did, and I liked his friends too. One day he invited me to come check out this team he was on. It was an AAU track and field team known as the Jefferson County Jets. Kids ages 6 and up could compete locally, regionally, and nationally in all sorts of running, jumping, and throwing events.

Jimmy's dad, Ike Jennings, who played briefly in the NFL for the Green Bay Packers, and his wife, Carol, always made room for me at their home. Coach Dick Cook, who lived down the street from them, was my first PE coach, and he was like the father I never had. Mr. Jennings and Coach Cook were the driving force behind the Jefferson County Jets in Crystal City. Coach Jon Bach, who lived in Crystal City but coached for Festus High School in the neighboring town, put in his time as well.

I didn't know it cost money to join the Jets. Joining fees were taken care of. Uniforms were provided.

Entry fees for races were covered. And Mr. Jennings and Coach Cook, along with other parents with kids on the team, always made sure I had a ride to and from the meets.

I'm thankful for the kids I grew up with, many of whom were also winners, state champions, and collegiate athletes. Marybeth Cook, Corky Hicks, and Greg Reecht: If you're reading this, then, yes, I'm talking about you.

I am and will forever will be grateful to Mr. Jennings and Coach Cook, because they (along with their families) created a pathway for me that I never realized, and probably wouldn't have ever known existed.

I'm thankful for track and field. I'm thankful for the opportunities it created for me, my friends, and all the other kids who needed a similar path.

God was looking out for me. He surrounded me with people who looked after me on his behalf and set me on a journey that has allowed me to meet amazing people and travel the world. He has used me as an instrument to help some young men and women become high school state champions, collegiate national champions, and Olympians. He has also used me as an instrument to help countless others earn better scholarships than they would have otherwise.

That invitation from Jimmy Jennings to go to the Jefferson County Jets AAU Track and Field team practice that day was a pivotal point in my life, and I had no idea how much of an impact it would have. I'm hoping that the knowledge, experience, and perspectives I've accumulated after a lifetime of being involved in track and field can create an equally pivotal point in the lives of other young men and women who have the talent and desire to compete in college and earn a scholarship. It is for those kids and their families that the following pages were written.

SECTION 1: LESSONS YOU DON'T WANT TO LEARN THE HARD (AND EXPENSIVE) WAY

It happens far too often. A great student, a great athlete, or a great student-athlete misses out on the scholarship that would have given them the education they needed without going into massive debt.

I don't care how much athletic talent an individual has, and I don't care what sport is being played. If athletes don't know the rules of the game they are playing, it can be ugly.

Well, the process of college recruiting is a game, and there are rules. When parents and the student-athletes they are trying to help get a paid spot on a college roster don't know the rules of the recruiting game, they lose.

I wrote this book to level the playing field. I want parents, students, and coaches to treat each other fairly and end up with the right kids on the right rosters with scholarship packages that give everyone the most value for their dollar.

Before I get into the nuts and bolts of the college recruiting process, I wanted to share a few true stories of athletes and parents who made some expensive and soul-crushing mistakes. These are just a few examples, but they are stereotypical and representative of the kind of mistakes I have seen happen year after year. I wrote this book so you don't have to suffer unnecessarily and can instead learn vicariously through the trials and tribulations of those who took these preventable missteps.

"Weighing His Options"

There was a high school hurdler who was one of the top three hurdlers in his state. He could run 300 meter hurdles in well under 38.20 and had one heck of an open 400 meter time too. He wanted to run for a Division I program and was being recruited by plenty of them.

The problem was that even though his GPA was solid, his best ACT score was too low. Unfortunately, to be Division I eligible at that time, he needed both a higher score on his ACT and a specific GPA in his core classes. He was, however, eligible for a Division II program, because there was a sliding scale and his ACT score combined with his GPA in high school was good enough to meet the Division II standards.

When he was offered a full scholarship by one particular Division II coach, he said he wanted to "weigh his options." Well, he weighed his options until the last day of the signing period and then called the coach back (at almost the last minute) to see if the offer was still on the table.

The answer was yes and no. Unfortunately for that athlete, waiting cost him $3,000, and while his scholarship was still significant, it was not a full scholarship because what remained was all that the coach had left to offer. He was truly fortunate to get what was left over. The answer could have been a straight no.

Had the athlete and/or his parents done their homework and known the rules, they wouldn't have wasted their time (or the coaches' time) targeting programs the athlete wasn't qualified to get into. Or they could have had him take additional ACT prep courses and retaken the test multiple times until he got an ACT score high enough to meet the Division I standard.

College-bound athletes entering school on or after August 1, 2016, were given new standards. It is a good idea to visit eligibilitycenter.org to familiarize yourself with the newest standards. These standards dictate the academic rules that must be met in order to receive scholarships, practice, or compete during the first year. Not knowing the rules can lead to costly mistakes.

"Didn't Know What He Didn't Know"

A 10.5 100 meter sprinter got a Division II full scholarship offer during the early signing period in the fall and turned it down because he was waiting for a Division I football scholarship offer.

Here's the problem. This young man had not spoken with any college football coaches. He had not visited any schools. The early signing period for track passed in November and the football season was over.

Granted, the signing period for football had not passed yet (but was close), but this kid had gotten exactly zero calls about his football ability. He turned down a full scholarship.

Again, this athlete did not understand how things worked. His parents did not understand how things worked either, and it was a horribly expensive way to find out.

"Windows of Opportunity Can Close Quickly"

A female who ran a sub-2:18 800 meter run and a sub-5:09 mile her junior year of high school track went on to compete in summer track meets organized by USA Track and Field (USATF). She traveled the country, ran outstanding times, and placed very high against top competition.

Following her performances at the USATF meets, she had lots of coaches calling her, emailing her, and texting her. She responded to exactly none of them and waited a month after her races were over. Even though she had a 3.8 GPA and a 27 on her ACT, coaches' interest in her cooled because of her lack of responsiveness.

When cross country season came along, she battled injuries and ended up being the second-best runner on her high school team, and her times were quite pedestrian and unimpressive compared to what they should have been.

One coach reached out to her after her dismal cross country season and was prepared to offer an outstanding scholarship. She was invited onto campus and accepted the invitation.

However, a few days before the official visit, she called to cancel because she wanted to attend the funeral of one of her high school acquaintances. It wasn't the death of her mom, dad, brother, sister, cousin, or grandparents. It wasn't even her best friend.

The moral of this story is to strike while the iron is hot, because the window of opportunity can close quickly. Not everyone is given a second chance. She was given a second chance when she was invited onto campus, but she blew it when she failed to grasp the importance of canceling her only invitation to an official college recruiting visit.

The coach was dumbfounded that this recruit, who had received exactly zero offers, made the choice to cancel an official visit. She was not invited back onto campus, and as of the early signing date, she had received exactly zero scholarship offers.

"Go Fast or Stay Home"

A female state champion who ran a 13.6 100 meter hurdle and could long jump 20 feet 7 inches was highly recruited by numerous schools. She had her heart set on a school in the Southeastern Conference (SEC) and received a verbal scholarship offer and made a verbal commitment to attend that school.

Between the date of her verbal commitment and the official signing date she competed in some indoor track meets while she was grossly out of shape. The coach who had recruited her and made the offer lost complete interest after seeing her poor performances and stopped returning calls. He offered the scholarship money he promised her to someone else who he felt could do a much better job.

When the signing date came, she never received a Letter of Intent. The official offer never came and she was heartbroken.

She eventually did get an offer from a Division I university out West, but it was not the school of her dreams and she never really enjoyed the sport like she had in the past and never reached her true potential.

If I could go back in time and offer her advice, I would tell her to sign early and/or stay off the track unless she was prepared to compete at a high level and go fast.

"The Grass Isn't Always Greener"

One young lady who ran a 4:50 mile, 10:40 3200 meter, and 2:07 800 meter in high school was recruited into one of the biggest and most prestigious conferences in the country and became the freshman of the year in that major Division I conference.

However, she thought the coach was too hard on her, and she gave up a full scholarship after one semester to transfer to another school in an entirely different conference located halfway across the country. She failed to improve on any times she had achieved as a freshman at her second collegiate stop and ended up transferring a third time to a forgettable and underachieving program where her running career ended unceremoniously.

Somebody somewhere along the line should have told that young lady that the grass isn't always greener in other pastures. Had she just stuck it out and been willing to learn and grow from her trials and tribulations instead of running from them, I think her story might have turned out differently.

At the very least I think athletes should stick it out for a full year before they contemplate the idea of transferring. Sometimes the change goes from bad to worse, and kids often don't realize how good they had things until it is too late.

"The Myth of Individualized Coaching"

One young man was one of the most decorated high school decathletes in the country. During each summer of his high school career, he had been developed and groomed through AAU and USATF competitions. Top college coaches had been watching him grow and improve year after year.

His club coaches got to know him and leveraged their relationships with college coaches to create multiple options for him; they worked hard to help line up what I considered the perfect place for him to go.

After a college visit he was offered an outstanding scholarship by the coach, but his parents told that coach "no thank you" because they thought there were too many decathletes on the team and they wanted their son to have individual coaching.

Their son still got a decent scholarship, but he ended up having to come up with about 30% of the cost of college per year. Those parents were naive and didn't realize that there really isn't any such thing as individualized coaching at that level. It's not like their son was going to become a professional decathlete because of some mythical type of "individualized coaching," and the bottom line was that over the course of four years, they would end up paying for more than one year of college. It didn't have to be that way.

College programs don't have an individual coach for each athlete. Kids are nurtured and mentored at the collegiate level, not individually coached. Remember that.

"The Money That Never Came"

One coach I know went to visit a young recruit and his parents at the young man's house. The coach had done his homework and the kid had impressive times and was deserving of a full scholarship based on merit. The coach walked into the house that day completely prepared to offer a full scholarship.

It didn't happen, and here's why: The parents made the mistake of opening their mouths and letting the coach know that their kid was coming to that school no matter what. They told the coach that their kid had money coming in from grandparents, from academic scholarships, and from savings that were set aside a long time ago.

Why the parents felt compelled to tell the coach all about the money they had coming in is still a mystery to me. I don't know if they thought they were impressing the coach or what. But right there, the coach decided to offer only 30% and use the other 70% he was going to offer that kid to help attract other athletes who needed it more in order to join his team.

As it turned out, the money the parents thought was coming didn't, and the kid who could have had a full scholarship ended up not being able to attend and had to settle somewhere else.

Telling coaches how much money you have doesn't impress them. Fast times and great marks impress coaches. When parents or kids tell coaches they are coming "no matter what," it is basically telling the coaches that they will take whatever they are offered even if it isn't much. When coaches realize they don't have to offer a lot to get an athlete, they won't offer nearly as much as they would have otherwise.

"Over Before It Started: The Abrupt End to a College Career"

Once, a female heptathlete from another country was in her college coach's office because the coach had asked to see her schedule so he could plan time to work with her on the high jump and shot put.

She promptly informed him that she wasn't going to do the high jump. When she arrived at practice, she informed him again that she wasn't going to high jump.

The coach picked up the phone and called her mom and told her he was putting her daughter on a plane that night to send her home, and that because of her insubordination her scholarship was being revoked.

The next day, the other kids at school from her country, of which there were quite a few, along with a few other coaches, asked him to attend a group meeting, and they set out to make a point and convince him he was wrong.

The coach listened to what they said and pointed at each one of them, along with the coaches who supported the insubordinate athlete who lost her scholarship and got sent home. The coach told them he was leaving the gym and they could follow him out the door and grab their stuff, too.

These kids were all on scholarship, and finding other athletes to replace them who were coachable and willing to take money to go to school wasn't a problem. The coach took a hard-line approach because no athlete is bigger than the program and it's wrong to back up someone who is wrong—in this case a scholarship athlete who is refusing to do what is asked.

The coach didn't make it more than five steps toward the door before they came running up begging him to change his mind and let them keep their scholarships and jobs. The coach is the boss, and it is important to remember the significance of doing what is asked.

Now that you have an idea of what not to do, let's talk about the recruiting process and how to create more and better scholarship offers by doing things the right way.

Section 2: How to Market Your Athlete to Coaches

Athlete Promotion: The 10-10-10 Plan

Where should parents and their student-athletes begin the process?

The first thing parents need to realize is that it is their responsibility to market their student-athlete. As Steven Covey once said, "Begin with the end in mind." You have to decide on what you want, put together a plan, and execute it in a way that creates as many satisfactory options as possible.

I have what I call the 10-10-10 plan. Both the parents and the student-athlete need to have a basic understanding of the student-athlete's career interests and realistic abilities. Then they need to establish some basic parameters for their ideal school (like cost, location, and degrees offered), and each needs to identify 10 colleges they think would be a good fit for the student-athlete.

For example, I have an athlete on our roster who said he wanted to go to school in Missouri or a surrounding state. He was interested in things like exercise science, physical therapy, and pre-chiropractic. His parents gave him an idea of what their budget was, and they each did their research to find schools their son realistically had the ability to compete for, schools that offered the desired majors, were in the designated geographical region, and were within their budget.

Of course there was some overlap, but the point is that once each of them assembled their list of 10 schools, they combined all their lists to create one final target list. Then they went to the websites for all of the colleges and found the contact information for the coaches. They also made sure that the performance marks of their student-athlete were competitive with the needs of the programs they were considering. Some schools had a link on their website especially for recruits, along with a questionnaire. Others listed the coaches' email addresses.

Building the 10-10-10 List: Doing the Homework

When selecting schools to target, it is critical that parents and athletes do their homework before reaching out to any coaches. For each school on their list of targets, they need to look at the university's website and see how their high school student's times and performances stack up against athletes who are already on the college roster. One of the main questions coaches are asking themselves when they evaluate potential athletes is this: Can this potential athlete help improve our team and score points at the conference championship?

If a recruit isn't capable of outperforming athletes already on the college roster and beating athletes from other schools at the conference championship, then they are of little value to the team, and expecting any significant athletic scholarship offers is unreasonable and unrealistic.

However, if a recruit is capable of improving a roster and can produce performances at the conference, regional, or national level of competition that will score points for the team, then it is likely the recruit can earn an athletic scholarship offer.

If high school athletes and their parents are not investing the time that is necessary to research and understand the performance standards and marks required to be competitive at the Division I, II, or III level (or smaller), then they are simply wasting their time, their kid's time, and a coach's time.

Building the 10-10-10 List: Performance Standard Benchmarks

While each university has different standards, the following should give you a ballpark idea of what typical minimum walk-on standards might be for a large Division I track program. These marks or similar performances may earn little to no athletic scholarship money at a large Division I program but could be enough to earn a partial scholarship at a smaller Division I program or a full scholarship or something close at many Division II schools.

<u>Women</u>

100m: 11.7

200m: 24.5

400m: 55

800m: 2:16

1600m: 5:15

3200m: 11:15

100m Hurdles: 14.10

300m Hurdles: 43

400m Hurdles: 63

Long Jump: 18 ft. 6 in.

Triple Jump: 38 ft.

Pole Vault: 12 ft.

High Jump: 5 ft. 8 in

Shot Put: 43 ft.

Discus: 155 ft.

Javelin: 130 ft.

Hammer: 120 ft.

Heptathlon: 4,630 points

Men

100m: 10.7

200m: 21.5

400m: 48

800m: 1:55

1600m: 4:18

3200m: 9:25

100m Hurdles: 14.2

300m Hurdles: 38

400m Hurdles: 53.5

Long Jump: 23 ft.

Triple Jump: 47 ft.

Pole Vault: 16 ft.

High Jump: 6 ft. 8 in.

Shot Put: 60 ft.

Discus: 180 ft.

Javelin: 180 ft.

Hammer: 170 ft.

Decathlon: 6,200 points

Building the 10-10-10 List: The Small Fish in a Big Pond Dilemma

When compiling a list of schools to target, parents and student-athletes should keep a few things in mind when it comes to the debate on big-name programs vs. smaller school programs. If a recruit can earn a full ride to a big-name program and score points at the conference, regional, or national level right away, that's great.

For everyone else, the big choice usually comes down to whether an athlete wants to be a small fish in a big pond or a big fish in a little pond. At the Division I level, everyone is an amazing athlete. For all but an elite few, kids who were state champions in high school might find themselves competing as an average or below average athlete when they first enter college.

Kids who were used to reading about themselves in the paper, answering reporters' questions in interviews, and winning their events suddenly become "average joes" or outright nobodies. This might last, in some cases, for a few years. After a few seasons of disciplined and focused training, they might get some taste of the kind of success they enjoyed as a high school athlete. But it takes lots of effort and time.

For example, a recent large-school state high school track and cross country champion—who even broke state records—found himself finishing in the middle of a 400-person Division I cross country race as a freshman.

Not every kid who has talent, works hard, and is used to winning can continue enjoying their sport when they get crushed week after week and month after month in races. Or what if they don't make the traveling roster? What if they don't even earn the privilege of competing in meets? How are they going to feel about sitting back at their dorm room when their teammates are out there doing what they love to do? When kids no longer enjoy their sport and the positive experiences it used to bring them, they may quit altogether, and then the scholarships stop help paying the bills.

I think it is better for kids to go where they can set realistic goals, develop, and do so in a way that fuels their competitive fire. There are plenty of outstanding athletes who can and will push each other at the Division II, Division III or National Association of Intercollegiate Athletics (NAIA) level as well.

When future employers see "NCAA All-American" on a kid's resume, they know the kid was an outstanding athlete regardless of the size of the school they competed for. Those employers realize that the athlete had the ability to effectively and realistically evaluate their abilities as well as their opportunities and make the most of each.

Unfortunately, I see far too many kids take their lumps for three years, hoping—often unsuccessfully—that they will develop into a winning Division I athlete by the time they are seniors. Too many kids and their parents drink the

"Kool-Aid" offered by the coaches of big-name programs and end up graduating college with a significant amount of student loan debt that could have been avoided considerably, if not entirely in some cases, had they targeted programs more suited to their talents and ability to contribute to the success of a particular college's program.

Whatever "prestige" an athlete receives from competing for a big-name program may feed their ego, but bigger and better scholarship offers from smaller, up-and coming-programs in schools that want to win can feed the stomach and pay the bills.

There are also plenty of success stories of kids who went to a smaller Division I school, a Division II school, or a private college and got a great education, were surrounded by like-minded peers who also set big but achievable goals, and contributed to a supportive and healthy academic and athletic environment.

These kids weren't just another face in a classroom; they got recognition on their campuses as well.

They understood the trade-off between the bragging rights of saying they competed for a big program and not paying much or anything for college. Because of their choices, they didn't have to start their adult life behind the eight ball due to the burden of student debt.

I tell everyone who will listen that the recruitment process is about the fit and about the money. Some folks think that there is no value to something you don't pay for. But when it comes to college and scholarships, I don't think there is anything that is further from the truth.

Please understand that the cost of a college education these days often tops six figures. When you add the cost of interest over the lifetime of the student loan, you realize those expenses climb even higher.

If you and your student-athlete do your homework, ask the right questions, and make the right choices, then when your child graduates, they will begin their adult life with some huge advantages.

They will develop marketable skills, be well travelled, and have established contacts. They will understand goal setting and teamwork. They will know how to handle adversity and overcome it. They will not have the added burden and pressure of paying off debt that rivals some families' home loans before they even start their first "real job" out of college.

The school where I coach is in a major metropolitan area. We have affluent, successful, and well-connected alumni who follow our athletes and teams on social media, and they follow the news on the university's website and the local news as well. They become familiar with these young men and women as well as their achievements. When our student-athletes are successful, they appear in Google searches, and future employers know they are winners.

If you were an employer and did an online search about a potential job applicant and found all kinds of positive things listed about one applicant and little or nothing about another applicant, who would you feel more comfortable about hiring? Would you be inclined to take your chances and roll the dice on an unknown, or would you take the winner with a proven track record of handling pressure, time management, and leadership?

Parents and athletes need to realize that this whole process is about getting an education, personal growth, and eventual job opportunities. Doing so with minimal debt is a huge advantage. It is a mistake, in my opinion, to keep some of the smaller schools off the initial 10-10-10 target list.

For sports such as football or basketball, the NCAA Division I almost serves as the minor league for professional sports. It's not necessarily the same for track and field and cross country.

In sports like football or basketball, where pro teams invest millions of dollars in draft choices, they want and need to see how an athlete compares to other elite talent under game pressures.

In track and field, or even cross country, there are time and distance marks, and the stopwatch and tape measure don't discriminate or play favorites. Either your student-athlete can hit performance standards or they can't. And it doesn't matter what team they are on or what it says on their jersey. The ability to hit those marks is worth different amounts of scholarship money to different schools.

<u>How do you initiate the process with a coach if you haven't ever heard from them?</u>

The bottom line is that it is the student-athlete's responsibility to market himself or herself. Once you've prepared a list of schools and coaches to reach out to (your 10-10-10 plan), it is important for the student-athlete to do four things.

1. Create a special email account for recruiting purposes only, review it regularly, and respond to inquiries immediately. Use good judgement in picking out a respectable username, too. Badboy123, BigBaller123, SexxxyRunnerGirl123, and similar names might make a memorable first

impression, but it will not be a good one. JohnDoeXC, JaneDoeVaulter, or JoeSmithThrower might be a bit more appropriate for this purpose. Also, it's a good idea to make sure the voicemail message set up for the student-athlete on their mobile phone is done in good taste and shows maturity and good judgement.

2. If an athlete wishes to compete at the Division I or Division II level, then they must register with the NCAA Eligibility Center. When you go to the website (www.ncaa.org), there will be an option for "play college sports" or "student-athlete registration" or something similar. The student-athlete or their parents can do this online, but the academic transcripts must be sent by the school, so it will be necessary to reach out to the high school counselor for assistance.

After registering, they must have their academic record and amateurism evaluated. Basically, the athlete needs to create a Certification Account on the website and submit the required forms along with the specific information requested on those forms. It is required that an athlete must create and complete a Certification Account before the athlete is allowed to make an official visit or sign a National Letter of Intent. It is recommended that student-athletes register with the NCAA Eligibility Center as early as the beginning of their sophomore year in high school.

Because Division III schools have their own eligibility requirements and standards, athletes who wish to compete in this division can create what is known as a free Profile Page. And if they decide to compete at the Division I or II level at a later date, they can and must transition to a Certification Account.

To receive an **academic certification**, the student-athlete must have submitted a final transcript as proof of graduation, along with transcripts from all other high schools they attended, and have no remaining academic tasks. A Division I or II school must also request that an evaluation gets completed by the NCAA Eligibility Center.

To receive what is known as **amateurism certification**, the student-athlete must accurately complete all of the questions related to sports participation. Spring enrollees can request final amateurism certification beginning on October 1. Fall enrollees can request final amateurism certification beginning on April 1.

If you need help during this process, then according to the NCAA site (as of the date of this publishing), customer service is available Monday through Friday from 9 a.m. to 5 p.m., and additional helpful information may be found at www.eligibilitycenter.org.

For Students and Parents with Eligibility Questions

877-262-1492 (toll-free)

International Students

NCAA Eligibility Center International Contact Form
317-917-6222

Transcript/Document Mailing Address

NCAA Eligibility Center
Certification Processing
P.O. Box 7136
Indianapolis, IN 46207

Overnight/Express Mailing Address

NCAA Eligibility Center
Certification Processing
1802 Alonzo Watford Sr. Drive
Indianapolis, IN 46202

Customer Service

9 a.m. to 5 p.m. Eastern Time, Monday through Friday
Fax number: 317-968-5100
Toll-free phone number (U.S. callers and Canada, except Quebec): 877-262-1492

3. Create a marketing portfolio. (To see a sample portfolio, visit www.CoachVinceBingham.com.) This is supposed to be a marketing piece that brings the student-athlete to life for recruiters. It is supposed to make the student-athlete stand out as more than a name, time, or mark on a database of competition results. It is a good idea to have a graphic designer do this, because you want it to look great. It is also a good idea to have someone else who is qualified to do so proofread it for errors. (As of the date of this writing, the folks at http://www.MaineProofreading.com are about as good as I have seen when it comes to proofreading.)

The portfolio should be anywhere from one to three pages in length depending on how much the student-athlete has accomplished. The first page should include an introduction, a few pictures, and top performance marks. The second page should be about athletics, and pictures are OK here too. The third page should be about academics. (And, yes, it is OK to have pictures here as well.) You don't have to fill three pages. If you can combine all this information on one to two pages, that's fine. As for general guidelines, some of the things the portfolio could/should include are:

<u>Name/Class Year</u>. The student-athlete's name and class year should appear in big, bold text at the top of the every page. It should stand out.

Introduction. This should be on page 1. It should say something like this:

Hello. Let me introduce myself.

My name is _____, and I am in _____ grade at _____ High School in ____ , _____. Currently, I am reviewing colleges and universities that could be possible choices for attendance in the fall of ____.

One of my goals is to compete in track and cross country at the collegiate level with the aid of a scholarship. The following pages contain information about my academic history and athletic performances.

If I can provide you with any additional information, please let me know. Thank you for your time and consideration. I look forward to hearing from you.

Sincerely,

_____ _____

<u>Top Performances</u>. Make sure the data are accurate and verifiable. For an athlete who has just completed his junior year, you might include something like the following:

Top Performances – Junior Year
2016 Cross Country – Top 5K Performance
15:44.2, Midwest Regional Championship

2017 Indoor Track Performances
4:23.51 – Mile – XYZ High School Invitational
9:31.59 – 2 Mile – University of XYZ High School Invitational

2017 Outdoor Track Performances

4:17.79 – 1600 – District XX Track and Field Championship

9:19.76 – 3200 – XYZ State Championship Meet

<u>Images (throughout the portfolio).</u> You should consider providing the following:

A. Competition pictures that feature the student-athlete. It is a good idea to select images that do not include other athletes. Don't give a coach a new reason to wonder who else is out there competing at a similar level.

B. Family pictures. Pictures with Mom and Dad supporting, encouraging, and/or congratulating the student-athlete may be included.

C. Other interests and activities. Pictures hiking in the mountains, swimming in lakes, dressed up for a dance, or having fun being a normal kid may be included.

D. Pictures of News Headlines. If you have images of news clippings with headlines of your student-athlete being recognized as "Athlete of the Week" or "Scholar-Athlete," you may consider including them (without the whole article).

<u>Athletic Development/Recognition.</u> You might include something like this:

Freshman Year: 2014-2015
-Varsity Letterman
-XYZ Town Athlete of the Week
-All Conference – All Academic

Sophomore Year: 2015-2016
-Varsity Letterman
-All District Cross Country
-All Conference – All Academic

Junior Year: 2016-2017
-XYZ Newspaper Athlete of the Week
-XYZ Radio Athlete of the Week
-All Conference – All Academic

-XYZ Town All Metro Team

-All Conference, Central Division Conference Champion

-All District – Cross Country, Track & Field

-All State – Cross Country

-Placed Xth – Class 4A State Cross Country Championships

<u>Contact Information</u>. You need to make it easy for coaches to reach either parent, the student-athlete, and their high school coach. For example, it is a good idea to include things like the following:

Contact Information:

John Doe (5'11"/128 pounds)

4153 Durham Drive

Anytown, MO XXXXX

JohnDoe@gmail.com

314-XXX-XXXX (mobile)

Father: Dad Doe

DadDoe@gmail.com

314-xxx-xxxx (mobile)

Mother: Mom Doe

MomDoe@gmail.com

314-xxx-xxxx (mobile)

Coach: Coach Michael Smith

314-XXX-XXXX (mobile)

CoachMichaelSmith@XYZHighSchool.com

XYZ High School

600 Main Street

Anytown, MO XXXXX

314-XXX-XXXX

<u>Academics</u>. This helps the coaches evaluate academic preparation for college. When they see what kind of classes a student-athlete has taken, what kind of grades they earned, and how they did

on standardized tests, such as the ACT, it will help them better evaluate how well a student is likely to do in the classroom.

For example, you might include something like the following:

Academics
Freshman Year: 2014-2015 GPA 4.0/4.0
-Biology I
-English I
-Freshman Health
-Honors Geometry
-Intro to Visual Design
-Spanish I
-Freshman Physical Education
-World Studies

Sophomore Year: 2015-2016 GPA 4.0/4.0
-Chemistry I
-Government and Politics
-Honors Algebra II
-Introduction to Mass Media

-English II: Literature and Composition

-Spanish II

-Cultural Foods

-Weight Training

-Personal Finance

Junior Year: 2016-2017 GPA 4.0/4.0

-Anatomy and Physiology

-Computer Applications

-American History (College Credit Course)

-English III: Literature and Composition

-Discrete Math

-Spanish III

-Physics I

ACT Composite Score: 23

Anticipated Major(s): Physical Therapy/Exercise Physiology

4. Send an introductory message that has been proofread (doesn't have a bunch of spelling or

grammatical errors). Use your own words, but here is a sample of what it should say.

Hello Coach _____,

My name is _____, and I am in ____ grade at _____ High School in _____, _____. Currently, I am reviewing colleges and universities that could be possible choices for attendance in the fall of ____.

One of my goals is to compete in track and cross country at the collegiate level with the aid of a scholarship. The attached pages contain information about my academic history and athletic performances.

If I can provide you with any additional information, please let me know. Thank you for your time and consideration. I look forward to hearing from you.

Sincerely,

_____

Phone: xxx-xxx-xxxx

Athlete Promotion: Online Matchmaking

What does online dating have to do with college recruiting? Nothing or everything, depending on your availability of time and money.

The dating world used to be pretty simple. Men and women used to meet at school, church, the supermarket, nightclubs, bars, workplaces, clubs, and groups created around special interests, usually located in the communities where they lived and worked. It took time to find out who was single and who wasn't available. It took time to find out which single people were even interested in dating. It took even more time to discover the background details that would contribute to the growth of a relationship or doom it before it ever really got started.

Using traditional dating methods, it took time to find out where people were from, what they were interested in, what activities they enjoyed, and what they did for work, and it was not only a time-consuming process, but also an awkward one for most. Let's face it, not everyone is comfortable initiating conversations with people they don't really know. The awkward introduction, the small talk, and the fear of rejection by either or both parties involved were more than enough to prevent the blossoming of romances otherwise capable of blossoming.

Now there are plenty of online Internet-based services like <u>match.com</u>, <u>PlentyOfFish.com</u>, <u>zoosk.com</u>, <u>eHarmony.com</u>, and others. For costs ranging from free to nominal, these sites now play the role of matchmaker. They promise to deliver a better-quality matchmaking process. These online services are designed for single men and women who are actively looking to meet other single men and women, so the question of whether or not participants are even interested in dating has already been answered. Participants create profiles including pictures, videos, and detailed descriptions about their likes, dislikes, wants, and needs in a relationship. The profiles are very detailed.

Once the participants create their profiles, it is easy to perform searches based on many different criteria including, but not limited to:

-Age

-Sex

-Location

-Earnings

-Hobbies

-Occupation

-Smokers/nonsmokers

-Number of kids

-Intent (marriage, casual dating, friendship)

-Relationship status (never married, divorced, widowed)

 Appearance (curvy, tall, athletic, thin, etc.)

-Religion (Baptist, Catholic, Jewish, etc.)

-Exercise frequency

-Educational level (HS, B.A., M.A., Ph.D.)

-Languages spoken

-Ethnic background

So, not only in theory, but in practice, a 35-year-old male who lives in St. Louis can find and get introduced to women according to his specific criteria. In other words, if he wants to meet females aged 30-40 who live within 20 miles of him and classify themselves as thin, he can do it. If he also wants to trim that list down to women who don't smoke, don't have kids, and earn over $50,000 per year, he can do it. If he wants to limit his list further to include only women who are Catholic and Hispanic, he can do it. When he has the list of people who meet his criteria, he is then able to review their pictures, videos, and detailed profile information. When he chooses the women he considers attractive and interesting, the dating sites make it easy (and safe, because people create usernames instead of their real names) to text or email an introduction. When the attraction is mutual, conversations begin to take place that otherwise wouldn't have. Relationships develop between people who are highly compatible that otherwise wouldn't have.

Here's what all this has to do with the recruiting process. Because coaches are looking for athletes and athletes are looking for coaches, I don't believe you *must have* an athletic "matchmaking" site to identify who is looking and who is available. However, I do see the potential for increasing an athlete's exposure beyond what the 10-10-10 plan can do. I also see potential time savings for an athlete and his or her family who use a service like what I'm about to describe in detail.

As of the date of this publishing, it is reasonable to expect that you will be asked to invest a minimum of close to $1,000 to use a service like the one below, but that investment might be insignificant relative to the additional scholarship money it could bring to the table that otherwise wouldn't have been available to you. It's a pretty simple concept, really. It's about connecting coaches who have scholarship dollars available with kids who want those dollars and have the performance marks and academic achievement to earn those dollars. When you have more coaches capable of finding an athlete who meets their criteria, the chances of that athlete receiving more scholarship offers are higher. When coaches have to compete against more other coaches to land the athletes they are seeking, the chances for higher offers increase.

Again, the 10-10-10 plan works just fine. Remember, I was talking about picking out no more than 30 potential coaches and finding their emails from their school websites and contacting them. The whole process takes a few hours. It also takes a few hours to create the portfolio. And a recruit still needs to register with the NCAA for eligibility. This works just fine in most cases. For everyone else who is interested in maximizing their options, the next level is using an additional service like the one at NCSASPORTS.ORG.

NCSA stands for Next College Student Athlete, and their site is not just for track and field and cross country athletes. Nor does it need to be, because the process of connecting coaches and athletes who meet each other's criteria is a fairly similar undertaking for most sports.

If you've created a portfolio, much of the work you've done for that can be copied and pasted into the athlete's profile at the NCSASPORTS.ORG site.

Profile information will include:

- Name
- Height
- Weight
- High school
- GPA
- Contact email
- Phone number
- Athletic history (years of participation, etc.)
- Key statistics (Pr's, etc.)
- Coach's name, phone number, and email
- Additional sports
- Athlete and parents' contact information
- Awards and activities

- Registration with NCAA Eligibility Center
- Highlights/skills video

The online profile also has room for the athlete to upload a picture, a personal statement, and a transcript.

One of the most useful features of the site, which may change but as of now is available for free to anyone who creates an account, is the College Search Map (located under the site's "Find Colleges" menu option). If an athlete performs a basic search, they can simply click on a state and it will show all the colleges in that state. It also displays information under Athletic Selectivity, Academic Selectivity, Division (I, II, III, etc.), Tuition (In-State), Tuition (Out of State), and Undergrad Enrollment. There is also a "match feature" that compares the athlete to the school, and an email option that allows the athlete to reach out directly to the registered contact person/coach at that particular college university.

The advanced search features are quite robust and easy to use as well. In addition to geographic searches, an athlete can narrow down a search based on the following categories:

-Collegiate Division

-Academic Selectivity

-School Enrollment (Specify: Minimum to Maximum Size)

-School Tuition (Specify: Minimum to Maximum Amount)

-School Type (Military, Women Only, Men Only, Christian, etc.)

-College Setting (Rural, Urban, Suburban, etc.)

-Public or Private

And last but not least is the ability to narrow down a search to colleges offering specific majors.

Even if an athlete doesn't pay for the membership to use the NCSA service, they can enjoy a huge time savings if they use the College Search Map feature to narrow down and create a list of the schools they might be interested in. Why bother looking at schools that don't have the degree offerings a student is interested in? Why bother looking at schools that are too big, too small, too expensive, too close, or too far away?

From the main dashboard, an athlete who has posted a profile can track:

- Profile views (number of times a coach has viewed an athlete's profile)
- Follows (number of college coaches who are keeping an athlete on their list of potential recruits)
- Email opens
- Searches (number of times an athlete came up in searches performed by coaches)

When an athlete pulls up what is called a "Coach's Activity Report," the athlete can see what state and what division the coaches looking at them are from. If an athlete thinks they are a definite Division I prospect and are only getting looks from NAIA or

Division III schools, the feedback becomes quite valuable.

The upside of expanding the visibility of an athlete using this process is the potential for receiving more scholarship offers and bigger scholarship offers. If a coach in New Hampshire finds a profile for an athlete who lives in Missouri (but is open to schools that far away from home), then new (and potentially lucrative) options become available to that athlete that otherwise wouldn't be.

There is a downside of being open to a large number of institutions if and only if an athlete makes themselves available to all of them. When the emails and phone calls come in to an athlete, they take time and effort to respond to appropriately and expeditiously. Remember that an athlete still needs time for school and for their training. Being overwhelmed by the additional responsibility of fielding and responding to an excessive amount of inquiries is a mistake and can be easily avoided.

ATHLETE PROMOTION: OFF-SEASON MEETS, CLUBS, AND ALL-STAR RACES

Beyond what they do while representing their school teams, what are some good ways to indirectly increase the visibility of athletes and help them earn the attention of coaches?

Not long ago, during a Christmas break, I ran into the father of an athlete who had begun making a name for himself in the St. Louis area at a restaurant, and we struck up a conversation.

I asked him how the college search was going for his son, who was in the middle of his junior year. He said it was fine.

I asked him what his son was doing for training during the off-season to get ready for his upcoming track season. He told me his son was running in a thing called the Frostbite Series, which is a winter series of long-distance races every other week or so with distances ranging anywhere from 7 to 13.1 miles in length.

Then I asked him why. He told me his son wanted to get in a lot of miles, stay in shape, and race because he loved the competition.

Then I asked him who saw the results of those races. The answer wasn't the college coaches at the universities his son was interested in attending.

The dad asked if I had any better suggestions, and I did. Since his son was intent on attending a university in Missouri or a surrounding state, I told him that he should enter his son in indoor track meets in Missouri and surrounding states. I made the case that not only would his son get to race against outstanding competition, but, more importantly, he would catch the eyes and attention of the coaches who were there as well as the ones who were actively monitoring the results of those meets.

While the coaches his son was interested in running for weren't paying attention to local road race results, they were paying attention to and attending the more prolific indoor track meets. The dad listened to my advice and his son changed course immediately. His son ran in meets in Arkansas, Missouri, Kentucky, and Tennessee, and it paid off. He received significant scholarship offers from coaches who saw him run in those indoor meets, too, which he might not have gotten otherwise.

Besides, when kids travel and step up against the best competition, it sends a message to the coaches about which kids are serious and passionate about their sport. It shows a much higher level of commitment.

It is important for kids to get out of their local area. The local area is too small of a box. If a talented athlete doesn't venture away from home much, if any, the local university knows they have the athlete locked up, and they won't throw out great offers because they know they have little or no competition. The local university isn't as likely to make a great offer simply because they don't have to.

When I was a kid, I ran for the Jefferson County Jets in the Festus/Crystal City area about 30 miles south of St. Louis, Missouri. There were other AAU and USATF teams in the area, too. In fact, club teams are all over the country and a good one is not hard to find.

I encourage recruits to join a club team and run track in the summer. I encourage them to get into off-season indoor track meets between cross country season and track season as well. Simply put, college coaches aren't scouring local 5k road race results. Athletes can improve their ability to attract more high-quality scholarship offers when they get some good marks and fast times listed in the meet results that coaches actually see.

I also encourage kids to race in select meets and all-star meets whenever they can. One of the kids we recruited for our current team raced indoor track at the University of Arkansas, the University of Kentucky, and Vanderbilt. Yes, he had to travel. But he got to race against nationally ranked athletes. He got great experience, and it built his confidence. He also got the attention of numerous college coaches.

In the select and all-star meets, he had to submit the times of his best recent performances to earn the privilege of racing. In the select meets, they only took the 30 fastest entrants. Some other meets were "all-comer" meets where everybody got to race. Granted, the athletes were seeded in each heat based on their previous times so they had people at or near their ability to race against, but everyone got to race. So there are select meets and there are "All-Comer" meets that make it possible for any kid to get an opportunity to race.

Make no mistake, coaches pay attention to the race results from these meets. When they see kids who are training and racing competitively in the off-season, they know these kids are passionate and dedicated. When they see the results, they know they are talented.

Over the three- to four-year span leading up to an athlete's college recruiting season, I try to encourage kids to attend and compete in a West Coast meet, an East Coast meet, and another meet in the central part of the country. That way, the kids get exposed to coaches from all over the country, as well as talented competitors from all over the country, which will inspire them to keep training hard. When a kid only competes against others they can beat easily in their local area, it can sometimes be difficult to convey the importance of lots of quality training. However, when those talented kids find out that there are lots of other talented kids out there who are as good and often better than they are, it is an eye-opener and the kids learn the importance of working hard without having to be nagged about it.

I'm always a fan of a kid attending a camp to improve their skills. However, in the right circumstances, (i.e., an athlete really wants to go to the school where the coaches hosting the camp do their coaching and the athlete has the talent to contribute to the college team there), it can also be a way for an athlete to get a coach's attention and get the time necessary to start and build upon a good relationship. If an athlete is going to spend five days with a coach, make no mistake, that coach will really get to know that athlete.

As it relates to networking, that just happens if an athlete has done their homework, attends the right meets, and isn't afraid to walk up to a coach, introduce themselves, and shake the coach's hand. I think coaches appreciate courtesy, respect, and self-confidence.

If an athlete comes up to a coach at a meet, introduces themselves, shakes hands, and goes on to win their race, then that coach is likely to remember it. The next thing the coach is likely to do is go back to the office, look the athlete up, and see where the athlete is from and what kind of times and marks they've achieved. Mission accomplished.

Section 3: Q&A with the Coaches: Insider Secrets Revealed

What happens after coaches and athletes get introduced is a process where recruits and coaches both move from general interests and questions to much more specific ones. Each is trying to find out more about the other. Neither wants to make a mistake, waste time, or money.

When phone calls, emails, unofficial visits, official visits, and scholarship offers start taking place, there are some specific rules, terms, considerations, and circumstances that exist. Coaches know how the rest of the game is played. Unfortunately, recruits and their parents simply don't know what they don't know, and in many cases don't even know what questions they should be asking or red flags they should be looking for.

The rest of this book is meant to serve as a guidebook and reference manual to eliminate fear, confusion, and anxiety about how the rest of the recruitment process typically unfolds. When recruits are successful in earning multiple scholarship offers, the following information should help them better evaluate their choices and minimize their risks of unintentionally sabotaging them. The following questions are ones that are frequently asked or should be asked by recruits and their parents at some point before a final decision on where to go to school is made.

1. WHAT ADDITIONAL CRITERIA SHOULD WEIGH INTO WHETHER OR NOT A COLLEGE IS THE RIGHT CHOICE AND BEST FIT FOR A STUDENT-ATHLETE?

When multiple offers exist and a recruit is struggling to differentiate between several good options and ultimately decide where they would be the happiest, here are some factors worth considering, additional questions worth asking, and a few insights on why they might be important.

Location

A. Is the university near a major metropolitan area? If a student-athlete has a long trip home, it helps if there are major transportation hubs nearby such as railroad stations, bus depots, and airports. I know some parents are particularly fond of areas serviced by low-cost airlines such as Southwest.

B. Is the location safe? Some universities are located in the heart of big cities, where crime rates are higher. If your student-athlete is a long-distance runner and much of their training is expected to take place in areas plagued by crime, high automobile traffic, and polluted air, that's worth considering. Rural areas or smaller towns tend to have lower crime rates and more safe training options.

C. Is the climate conducive to effective and consistent training? If it is sunny and 70 degrees 10-12 months out of the year, the weather isn't a factor. If it is cold, wet, snowy, or icy most of the time, that can be a factor. If weather is not ideal, does the university have alternative/indoor training facilities that student-athletes can use instead?

D. Is the university close to home? If it is, then parents can expect to save significant money when it comes to travel. And, as a bonus, parents are typically able to attend more of their child's competitions. If the student-athlete wants to go far away from home, be sure to plan for extra expenses associated with travel.

E. Are there "cool factors" such as lakes, mountains, or oceans? It's nice for kids to have options when they aren't studying or training. A walk on the beach, a dip in the lake, or a hike on a mountain trail can be a great stress reliever, or an excuse not to go to class depending on how disciplined your student-athlete is.

Academics

A. Tutors – Find out if academic tutors are available to student-athletes and if there is an additional cost associated with those services.

B. Graduation rates – Ask what percentage of athletes who start with the program as freshman graduate and complete their degrees.

C. Teacher-to-student ratios – Ask about teacher-to-student ratios. Smaller teacher-to-student ratios often translate into more personal attention and better accessibility to professors if or when students need additional help or guidance.

D. Degree offerings – If a college or university doesn't offer majors related to the student-athlete's interests and abilities, it shouldn't make the list.

E. GPAs/majors of current athletes – If the team GPA is high and the kids are taking challenging majors, then academics are not an afterthought. If not, it might be wise to inquire as to why.

Cost

What is the most your family can afford/is willing to invest if a partial scholarship is all that is offered?

Career Development

Ask about the job placement and career services offered by the university. Find out what kind of opportunities exist for internships and networking with professionals outside of the classroom. A lot of times community service projects and cooperative programs between students and professionals in the workforce open doors for students that would otherwise be closed.

Coaching Staff

A. Pedigree

What have the coaches accomplished? What are their certifications and greatest achievements? Be sure to ask questions about the number of conference champions, All-Americans, and Olympians that have been through their programs.

Ask questions about performance improvement so you can get an idea how much athletes have improved their marks and times year after year. If you don't see significant and continual improvements, it might help to ask why. (If a number of athletes are injured frequently, ask why.)

What success has the university and each event coach achieved historically speaking?

B. Tenure

How long have the coaches been on staff? Inquire about their years of service in their current role as well as past roles. Ask why they left other positions. A younger coach may be looking to make a name for themselves at smaller programs so they can move on to something bigger and better as soon as possible. An older coach may want to ride out his or her career where they're at without uprooting their ties to the local area. If the student-athlete selects a program based heavily on the relationship with a particular coach, and the coach leaves, the student-athlete is linked to the university, not the coach.

Another sign of problems with a program's culture is a revolving door of assistant coaches. If assistant coaches come and go on a regular basis, it could be a red flag. It is a good idea to inquire about the tenure of assistant coaches.

C. Culture

Ask the coaches about their goals. What has to happen for them to feel a season was a success? Does the team have to win the conference championship? Does the team need to win the regional or even the national championship for the coach to feel like the season was a success? Or would the coach be happy just placing in the top half of the meets they compete in?

What kind of competition does the coach seek out for the kids? Are most, if not all, of the competitions and meets local ones, against weak competition? Are the competitors mainly from schools the same size or smaller? Or does the coach believe in traveling if necessary to test his or her athletes against bigger or historically better programs every time there is a chance to do so?

Rest assured, coaches want to know if a student-athlete thinks big and is committed to high standards. Turnabout is fair play. Parents and student-athletes need to know how important winning and continual improvement is to the people doing the coaching. They also need to know how important academic achievement is to coaches.

If there are a lot of injuries, it could be a red flag. It's not like track and cross country are contact sports. If there are lots of kids walking around using boots or crutches, ask why. If there are several athletes with similar injuries, like stress fractures, for example, then it is probably not a problem related to a particular athlete or two and is more likely an indictment of the training program the kids are on. If you see current athletes with eating disorders, then that is a red flag about the program.

Some coaches don't want to admit it, but the hard truth is that in some programs, winning is everything and academics are not the #1 priority. I like to think that academics are still the #1 priority for most coaches, but rest assured, if a student-athlete is on scholarship, athletic success is very close in importance.

Ask current athletes what their coach would say if they asked to skip practice to study for an important test or to finish an important paper. Ask current athletes if they are pushed to compete while injured. The answers to those questions can give you a good feel for the values and priorities of a coaching staff.

Finally, what is the composition and makeup of the team (local, regional, or international)?

D. Philosophy

What are the coach's thoughts on doubling up and/or multi events?

What are the coach's thoughts on summer meets?

What kind of coaching will the student-athlete receive during competition?

How does the coach feel about participation in international meets or on national teams (Olympics, etc.)?

How many events are coached by a coach?

What is the coach's redshirt policy?

How does the team usually travel to competitions (air, bus, van, etc.)?

How often does the team compete, and how far do they travel? (Take a look at the schedule and locations of meets for the last five years to get a feel for it.)

How many athletes does a team have on a roster for the event your student-athlete is being recruited for, and what are their class ranks?

What are the coach's thoughts/policies regarding holiday breaks?

What are the coach's thoughts on summer school, and are summer classes covered by scholarship offers?

What is the coach's post-collegiate philosophy? In other words, how does the coach feel about graduates who want to come back and coach or be coached if they have aspirations like the Olympics?

How would a coach describe their ideal coach-athlete relationship?

How would the coach describe their training philosophy?

How does the coach use technology (film, etc.) to individualize training, improve technique, and execute strategy?

How would the coach describe their role or the university's role in teaching life skills and career development?

<u>Scholarship Renewal Policy</u>

What is the scholarship renewal policy?

<u>Health/Injury Prevention/Rehab</u>

How many full-time trainers are on staff?

How experienced are the trainers on staff?

Who are the team doctors, and how accessible are they?

What are the training room hours of operation?

What are the injury statistics?

How many injuries have occurred?

What kind of injuries were they?

How serious were they, and how long did it take for the athletes who were injured to return to competition?

What services were they offered (physical therapy, chiropractic, massage, etc.)?

What kind of alternative training was prescribed?

Campus Life/Living Arrangements

There are lots of important questions to ask about living arrangements and options. Having the answers to the following questions will serve you well:

How many roommates will the student-athlete have, and how are they selected?

What housing options exist, and how do the coaches and teammates feel about each of them?

-Dorms (Co-ed or not? Visitation policies?)

-Fraternity/sorority houses

-Off-campus apartments

-Access to public transportation

-Distance from classes

-Distance to the airport

-Additional costs

How safe is the area, and what kind of security measures are in place?

Are cars allowed, and what is the availability of parking?

What is the population of the school?

What is the culture of the university?

What are the facilities like (new, modern, good quality)?

Team Travel Budget and Equipment Policies

As of the writing of this book, there are some states who are experiencing a significant budget crisis. Huge cuts are being made to education. This means a lot to a student-athlete who attends a university tied to those budget cuts. For example, if travel budgets are cut, they may be limited to competing in far fewer events, closer to campus where competition is greatly reduced. If a student-athlete is part of a program that gets cut, they do have the option of remaining at the university on scholarship, but they won't have a team to compete with or for unless they want to transfer. Or the university may choose to release them from their scholarship and allow them to go compete at another school.

Find out what allowances, if any, are made for shoes, uniforms, and training gear. What costs are the responsibility of the student-athlete? What costs are picked up by the athletic department and team? A long-distance runner who trains an average of 75 miles a week and gets 350 miles per pair before wearing them out will go through 11 pairs of shoes in a year. At $125 per pair, that's another $1,375 per year in expenses.

2. WHAT IS THE AVAILABILITY OF THE COLLEGE SCHOLARSHIPS A STUDENT-ATHLETE IS COMPETING FOR?

NCAA Division I

Currently at the Division I level, each college and university is limited in their ability to offer no more than the equivalent of 12 full athletic scholarships to men and no more than 18 full athletic scholarships to women to field a team. The amounts can be broken up, though. For example, a university could also offer up to 24 half-scholarships to male athletes and 36 half-scholarships to female athletes. The bottom line is that they can break down the scholarship dollars however they choose as long as the total amounts don't exceed 12 full scholarships for men and 18 for women.

NCAA Division II

Currently at the Division II level, each college and university is limited in their ability to offer no more than the equivalent of 12 full athletic scholarships to men and no more than 12 full athletic scholarships to women. The amounts can also be broken up to offer a greater number of smaller scholarships.

NCAA Division III

Currently at the Division III level, athletic scholarships are not offered per se.

NAIA

Currently, at the NAIA level, each college and university is limited in their ability to offer no more than the equivalent of 12 full athletic scholarships to men and no more than 18 full athletic scholarships to women.

Junior Colleges

Currently junior colleges have the ability to offer partial scholarships at their discretion.

So, what does all this mean for student-athletes and their parents? If a student-athlete is looking at joining a large team, that means there are a lot of kids dividing up available scholarship dollars. If there are 60 men on a track team and there is only enough scholarship money to cover 12 full scholarships, that means there aren't a lot of people getting a full ride.

Parents in a situation like this are wise to look at all the costs and decide if they can afford to cover a third, a half, or more of the likely expenses associated with their student-athlete making the choice to attend that particular college or university.

If your family earns even a modest income, qualifying for government grants may be out of the question.

3. WHAT ARE SOME OF THE ADDITIONAL OR INTANGIBLE THINGS THAT IMPACT A COACH'S IMPRESSION OF A STUDENT-ATHLETE?

Coaches want to be impressed by maturity, responsibility and responsiveness. They want to know that a student-athlete has a sense of personal responsibility.

Does the student-athlete take care of business when asked? Or do they have to be reminded and waited on? Coaches don't want to have to babysit young adults; they want to lead and develop them. They don't want to have to wonder or worry about whether or not a student-athlete will make it to practice on time or at all. They don't want to wonder or worry about whether or not their student-athlete will miss the bus to competitions. They don't want to have to hold anyone's hand to get them to go to class regularly and study enough to make good grades.

They want to see discipline. They want to see commitment. They want to see polite kids with good manners.

Coaches want kids who can put their phone down long enough to carry on a fully engaged conversation without being tempted to look at, much less respond to, an incoming phone call or text message.

4. How do coaches evaluate the intangibles they are looking for?

It is to be expected that coaches will do their homework on a recruit before making significant scholarship offers.

<u>Social Media</u>

Coaches will look up athletes on social media. They want to see how a recruit dresses, how they act, how they talk, and what they talk about.

They are looking for signs of bad judgement and the potential for future problems. The words the kids use, the topics they discuss, and the images they choose to portray themselves with carry a lot of weight with most coaches.

If a kid feels comfortable showing pictures from drug and/or alcohol parties while they are underage or uses insensitive and/or profane language, otherwise good scholarship offers can be significantly reduced or blown completely.

High School Coaches

Expect college coaches who are interested in a particular student-athlete to reach out to their high school coaches and ask all kinds of questions. Of course they will ask questions about training and performance improvement. But it is also reasonable to expect them to ask questions about leadership, self-discipline, respect of the athlete's peers, and more.

Peer Evaluations

During official visits, prospective athletes often spend the night on campus with the current athletes who would be their future team members. The coaches schedule things like dinner with the parents and teammates. They schedule activities like laser tag, bowling, movies, or other fun things so the recruit has a good time and the athletes on the current roster have a chance to get to know the recruit, too.

Of course the coaches want the recruit to have fun and feel comfortable with all their potential teammates. But they also want to know how the recruits act when they think the coach isn't watching. Make no mistake, coaches will ask the team members all kinds of things about the recruit. If all the recruit wanted to do was get drunk, do drugs, cause trouble, or try to pick up a one night stand, then the coaches are able to avoid future problems before they occur by offering scholarships to other kids who have values more aligned with their goals.

Competitors

It is very likely that the coaches are also talking to similar-caliber athletes who compete against each other. During recruiting visits, it is not uncommon for coaches to ask athletes how well they know each other and what they think of each other. Let's just say it pays for a student-athlete to be a nice person and tough competitor.

5. WHAT SHOULD RECRUITS SAY OR DO IF OR WHEN THEY FEEL PRESSURED TO ENGAGE IN RISKY BEHAVIORS OR FEEL LIKE THEY MIGHT BE GETTING TESTED ON A RECRUITING TRIP?

The bottom line is that if a recruit is ever put in a compromising position, it might be a test.

Either way, the best thing a recruit can do is say something like "No thanks; I'd prefer to do something different, like x, y, or z."

In some cases it might not be a test, and maybe the school recruiting an athlete actually has a team that's full of partiers and troublemakers. It happens.

One of the most highly sought after pole vaulters in the nation had the opportunity to go to pretty much any college he wanted to. Everyone wanted this guy. He was the best and everyone knew it.

When he came back from college visits, he talked about all the girls and partying. When people asked him why he chose the college he finally settled on, they wanted to know why.

In no uncertain terms, he told them. "I don't drink. I don't smoke. I don't do drugs. I don't stay out late or party. To wind down, I'd rather play a few video games or something with a few buddies. I picked a college where I could focus on what is most important to me, and that is getting a great education and being the best pole vaulter I can possibly be."

He knew what his priorities were and found a place aligned most perfectly with them.

6. Are there any common pet peeves coaches have that recruits would be wise to be wary of?

Being respectful goes a long way. One of the best things a kid can do on a recruiting trip is put away his or her phone and give every single person they meet their undivided attention. They shouldn't respond to texts, pick up phone calls, or do anything that would make it look like they lack interest in anyone they met or anything they are doing. Along those same lines, it's a good idea to get a good night's sleep the night before a recruiting trip so the recruit doesn't ever yawn or appear disinterested.

When on a recruiting trip, act like you would if you were in church and it's hard to go wrong.

7. WHAT CAN A RECRUIT DO TO BUILD A CONNECTION WITH A COACH DURING THE RECRUITING PROCESS?

First of all, the recruit should demonstrate sincere interest. That can be accomplished easily by doing something as simple as sending email once in awhile (not every day or week) showing that the athlete is actively following and engaged in how well the college team did or particular athletes on their team did in a recent competition. It doesn't hurt to periodically keep the college coach abreast of how recent races have gone, what lessons were learned, and what improvements have been taking place.

You get bonus points for demonstrating faith in your coach and giving credit where it is due, and not making excuses when expectations aren't met.

It has to be sincere. Coaches will sniff BS a mile away.

It also helps to be responsive. An athlete that doesn't check or respond to emails ASAP is missing opportunities. If a coach asks for something and the athlete doesn't handle it right away, that's a mistake.

I recently asked a recruit if he had gone to the NCAA website and registered himself in their system. He didn't know he needed to do that but got right on it and called me the next day to let me know it was done. He was a state champion being recruited by numerous schools, but he acted fast, showed interest, and handled his business like a mature young man. What's not to like?

There are some nights when lots of coaches are calling and kids can get overwhelmed. Rather than look unresponsive or disinterested, it's a good idea for kids to be proactive and thank the coach for reaching out, and let them know they were studying for a big test or had a project due and would love to schedule time to talk.

Or if a coach calls for a visit and the timing is terrible, it's OK for a kid to tell the coach they really want to visit but have a test in the morning, project due, etc., and ask if there is another time they could visit. If the kid lets the coach know they are very interested and have a list of questions they would like to ask, I think most coaches understand and appreciate the sense of personal responsibility.

8. WHAT SHOULD A KID DO IF THEY'VE MADE SOME MISTAKES IN THE PAST SOCIALLY, ATHLETICALLY, OR ACADEMICALLY?

The best advice is to own the mistakes and accept the responsibility for making them and the consequences that followed. Then the student-athlete should talk about what lessons they learned as a result and what they are doing and will continue to do to move forward because of those teachable moments.

When I say own it, I mean own it. This is not the time to give some canned, politically correct BS that sounds good. This is the time to be vulnerable and sincere. When a kid comes out and says something like "I made a terrible choice to try and look cool in front of this girl I liked since first grade. All my buddies were pushing me to go with them to this party when I knew there would be people there using drugs. I was in the car when we got pulled over, and I won't ever let myself get talked into doing something I know is wrong no matter who is trying to talk me into it. I'm not hanging around those guys anymore, either. I needed to make some new friends, and I have."

If coaches can't trust a kid, most don't want them. Even after a heartfelt and sincere explanation, some coaches still might not be willing to take a chance. But if a coach really believes that a kid "gets it" and sees what they did wrong, understands why it was wrong, understands the consequences of what they did, and is taking active measures to avoid anything like that in the future, second chances are still possible.

9. CAN SCHOLARSHIPS BE TAKEN AWAY?

Yes and no.

Here's the "Yes" part of the answer.

The most common ways to lose a scholarship under NCAA rules is to for a student-athlete to render themselves academically ineligible or break a school rule or team policy. Flunk classes, get caught cheating, miss practices, miss competitions, or be disrespectful toward a coach and it can all be over.

Here's the "No" part of the answer.

Student-athletes cannot lose their scholarship because they got injured or weren't performing well. However, if a coach makes mention in conversation related to a reduction in scholarship, the student-athlete needs to make it a priority to do exactly what is asked in a respectful way. The student-athlete needs to show up early for practice each and every time and do whatever is asked of them. A coach might be looking for any little excuse, and the smart student-athlete won't give the coach that opportunity.

10. How should a parent and/or recruit handle it when a coach is trying to find out the answer to: "What other schools is the scholar-athlete being recruited by/looking at?"

Rule #1: Parents and recruits should never talk about another university or college when visiting a campus, unless they are asked directly.

Rule #2: It's best not to pick up the phone (because it could be another coach calling), and the host university and coach deserves respect.

Rule #3: When asked directly, it is best to be mindful of who is asking. At an NCAA Division I school, it's best to let the coach know that other Division I schools are showing interest.

At an NCAA Division II school, it's fine to mention other Division II schools as well. If the other Division II schools are in the same conference, it's even better.

A Division I program like the University of Missouri in the SEC isn't nearly as likely to compete as aggressively for a recruit being sought after by smaller schools they don't compete against, like Missouri Southern or Truman State University, as they would be if they knew their SEC conference rivals Alabama and Arkansas are in the mix. Coaches in Division I programs want athletes who are thinking big and looking (and being looked at) by other Division I programs.

Rule #4: Casting a big net and reaching out to a lot of college coaches can create lots of options and start bidding wars (which bring more and bigger scholarship offers), but when talking to coaches, it's best to mention only two or three. It is also important that the coach doing the recruiting believes their university is at or near the top of the list.

This is important for several reasons. Why? Because coaches don't want to waste their time on recruits who are long shots and relatively disinterested. They want passionate, committed athletes who are really interested in what their program offers. If coaches don't feel like their program is a front runner, they will move on and won't waste their time.

However, if coaches don't feel they have any competition and an athlete is dying to be part of their team, the possibility exists that they will offer a less-than-market-value scholarship offer. Why would they offer more if they don't think anyone is bidding against them?

The ultimate goal is to respectfully communicate that a bidding war is necessary so a market-value scholarship offer materializes, and that there is also a really good chance the scholarship offer will be accepted if it's made so the coach doesn't feel any time was wasted.

Rule #5: One of the first objectives is to get an offer from a school that is 2-3 hours away that is affordable. This is important because in future conversations with other coaches, the words "We've already received an offer of _____" alerts them to the fact that a bidding war has begun. Generally, if a recruit can get two or three schools in the same conference making offers, the offers will be better.

Rule #6: The coaches know each other and they talk to each other. I know that if I'm recruiting a kid and my university isn't the right fit and I don't think I can get this athlete regardless of how aggressive our scholarship offers are, I will call other coaches with programs that are better suited. If I have a good relationship with a kid and his or her family is polite, respectful, and appreciative, I will go out of my way to help that kid. If the kid has the talent, I will call coaches I know and tell them to take a look at this kid. They do the same for me.

11. WHAT HAPPENS IF A STUDENT-ATHLETE MAKES A MISTAKE AND WANTS TO TRANSFER?

This is more of an "after the fact" question, but I think it is important for kids to know that some mistakes made during the recruiting process can be undone. It takes some of the pressure off when they know that it's not the end of the world if they pick the wrong school the first time.

The best way to handle this situation is for a student-athlete to be up-front and respectful to their college coach and let them know that they miss home and want to go to school closer, or their academic interests are different from what they originally thought and want to be officially released and granted permission to talk to other schools so they can transfer. Nine times out of ten, a coach will grant that release waiver. And as long as the athlete was in good academic standing, they will be free to transfer.

If a release waiver is granted, athletes are allowed to transfer one time without being forced to sit out of competition for any length of time. However, if a release is not granted, the student is prohibited from competition for 365 days unless they are in the NAIA. Without a release, in the NAIA, athletes are prohibited from competition for only one semester.

12. HOW DOES SOMEONE KNOW IF THEY GOT A GOOD SCHOLARSHIP OFFER?

A full athletic scholarship means tuition, room and board, books, and fees. The reason coaches are most interested in "well-rounded" athletes (kids with good grades, high ACT scores, etc.) is that they can stack scholarships and financial aid to get these kids in school without wiping out their athletic scholarship budgets.

A kid might be able to go to school with no money out of pocket if half of the costs are covered by academic scholarships and half are covered by athletic scholarships. Or a kid might be able to get financial aid or student loans to make up the gaps not covered by scholarships. If the remaining gaps between what it costs to go to school and what's covered by scholarships and grants can be handled by the family, then it is a good scholarship offer.

Good students are particularly attractive to coaches because they don't have to worry about academic ineligibility. Coaches don't have to give up as much of their athletic budget and can use those dollars to attract additional talented athletes. And since coaches are evaluated on the team GPA and graduation rates just like they are on athletic performance, a 4.0 student contributes a lot to raising the team's GPA.

A good scholarship offer is one that makes it affordable to attend college. A great offer pays for most or all of it.

13. WHAT ARE SIGNING PERIODS, AND WHEN ARE THEY?

The signing date is the day that a formal contractual scholarship offer is made in writing from the college and is signed by the student-athlete. It is a binding agreement, and once it has been signed, the recruiting process for that student-athlete is complete and interaction with other colleges ceases.

There are two signing periods for cross country and track and field. One is known as the early signing period, and it is the second Tuesday of November. The late signing period is the second Tuesday of April.

In the early signing period, a student-athlete has 21 days to sign the financial aid agreement or National Letter of Intent. If they do not, then they need to wait until the April signing date.

14. What considerations factor into the decision of whether to sign during the early signing period or wait until the late signing period? What's the difference between written and verbal offers?

If a coach makes a good offer or even a great offer to a kid during the early signing period and the kid chooses to wait without committing, then some coaches will move on to their next choices, and depending on whether or not the other athletes being recruited accept their offers, the scholarship money that was available in November may no longer be available from that school in April to the same athlete.

The recruiting process can be stressful, and it is time-consuming, not only for the coaches, who still have to coach their teams, but for the athletes, who are getting all the phone calls and emails as well, while trying to keep their grades up and finish high school.

Some kids (and coaches) find it to be a relief when the deal offered is a good one and the athlete accepts it during the early signing period. If a kid really wants to attend a specific school and the offer is good, the advantage to accepting it is that the money is contractually guaranteed to be there and the kid can attend that school assuming the offer made it affordable.

The waiting game can be a dangerous game to play for a recruit. If a kid isn't getting a bunch of calls and invitations to visit campuses in September and October, then that kid is behind the eight ball. If the colleges are recruiting in November and they spend all their money, there might not be much, if any, scholarship money left to offer in the spring. Additionally, academic money is usually awarded by December, too. So, if academic scholarships are dried up and athletic scholarship dollars have been accepted by other athletes, then a recruit who waited might be out of luck. It is for those reasons, I believe, that the vast majority of recruits sign during the early signing period.

If the kid is open to several schools, isn't sure which one would be best, and could be happy at several places and is willing to risk getting fewer or smaller offers in exchange for the possibility of getting even bigger offers, then waiting it out until the spring can, in certain situations, make decent sense.

If a coach becomes the second choice of his or her top recruiting prospects and many of the kids the coach was counting on signing end up going elsewhere, a coach might be sitting on lots of scholarship dollars late in the recruiting cycle. The possibility exists that the coach might throw an even better offer to a kid in the spring than he or she would have in November if the dollars are still there and they are lacking a number of talented and committed athletes.

If a kid who didn't commit during the early signing period gets injured and/or performs below expectations in the spring, they might get fewer and worse offers. If they perform above expectations, they may get more and better offers if they wait until the late signing period.

There are risks and rewards associated with both the early signing period and the late signing period. It is important for parents and athletes to know the different risks, rewards, and consequences associated with their decisions.

Commitments made in writing on both the early signing date and late signing date are binding. But what about verbal offers and commitments made and accepted in between those two dates? Are they binding?

Scholarship offers following the early signing period are verbal ones. If a coach makes a verbal offer, it is important to know it is not binding. There are some coaches—granted, they are few and far between, but they do exist—who will make a verbal offer to a kid and renege if they can get what they think is a better student-athlete to commit leading up to the late signing period.

The good news is that most coaches will honor their verbal offers because they know that a reputation for misleading kids is not one that will serve them in the long term. But I do know of instances where a kid was waiting to get their written formal scholarship offer on the late signing date and it never came.

If a coach has a history of not honoring verbal commitments, other coaches will know it. And if the kid is a good kid and the parents are respectful and polite, I think most other coaches will give the parents a heads-up about that coach's history of pulling offers.

If communication from a coach to an athlete goes away, that is a red flag after a verbal offer has been made. If more than two or three weeks go by and a recruit doesn't hear something from somebody at that institution, and isn't in the system in any way, shape, or form, it could be the foreshadowing of bad news. The recruit should be hearing from admissions, the financial aid office, assistant coaches, or somebody from the institution every so often. If the recruit's phone calls, texts, or emails get ignored and nobody is responding, it's not a good sign.

In my estimation, 95% of coaches will honor their verbal offers, at least for a while. It's not uncommon for a coach to tell an athlete that they will hold a verbal offer open until a certain date before offering those scholarship dollars to another athlete who is willing to verbally commit to accepting a scholarship offer on the late signing date.

Equally, if a recruit makes a verbal commitment, that verbal commitment is not binding either. And other colleges will keep calling on a kid they really want. So, for example, if a kid gets and verbally accepts a 50% scholarship to attend one college and another college offers the kid a full scholarship before the late signing date, the student may accept it and back out of their prior verbal commitment.

Smart coaches will stay in touch and continue building relationships with the recruits who have given them a verbal acceptance of a verbal offer, because they know top recruits are still being called by other colleges and they don't want to lose them. Smart athletes, who don't want to risk having the dollars they were promised go to another athlete, are also wise to stay engaged in conversations with the coach during the time between the two signing dates.

I might suggest that the recruit stay in touch with the coach every two to three weeks or so and update the coach on training and race results. It's a good idea for the recruit to stay abreast of how the college team is doing and show interest in their future teammates' accomplishments as well. A simple email or text to the coach once in a while lets the coach know the kid is watching, paying attention, and still interested, even if the coach is also in season. Coaches like to know that a recruit is still invested.

Hard feelings can and often do occur when a coach breaks a verbal commitment to an athlete or when an athlete breaks one to a coach, but it can and does happen. It has been my experience that unless the verbal scholarship offers are vastly different, like going from a 25% scholarship offer at one college to a 100% offer from another college, most parents want to set an example a for their kids that giving your word means something, and they encourage their kids to honor their initial commitment. However, if a kid is able to get a dramatically better offer that cuts their cost of college down by a significant amount, like half, then most coaches understand that a recruit is simply doing what's best for themselves or their family, even if they don't like it.

15. WHAT'S THE BEST WAY TO ACCEPT A VERBAL SCHOLARSHIP OFFER AND MAKE A VERBAL COMMITMENT?

The recruit needs to pick up the phone and call the coach and let him or her know that their mind is made up, they want to attend that institution, and that they are grateful for the scholarship that was offered.

Regarding the coaches at other programs who also actively recruited that athlete, it is also a good idea to have the recruit pick up the phone and call the other coaches that were making offers and thank them for their time and interest. Let the other coaches know that their time and effort was respected and appreciated.

So that it isn't awkward, it's easy for the recruit to give a simple reason, like wanting to stay closer to home or another college having academic programs more closely aligned with their career goals. It doesn't have to be a long conversation, but it is polite to tell them a decision has been made to attend a different university, give them a decent reason, thank them for their time, and let them know that they deserved the courtesy of a call. In closing, it might not be a bad idea for the recruit to also let the coach know that if things don't work out as expected, they would like to keep the door open and be able to call down the road if possible.

Some coaches may be salty, and a few might even be rude. But the vast majority will appreciate and respect a young man or woman who takes the time to express appreciation and common courtesy.

And in the unlikely event that the coach at the program the athlete verbally committed to originally reneges on their verbal offer and gives it to someone else, a coach who liked and appreciated the way a young man or woman respectfully declined their scholarship offer might be willing to extend another offer if they still have scholarship money available.

It's smart not to burn any bridges and leave doors open whenever you can. Besides, if things don't work out as originally planned and an athlete wants to transfer down the road, make no mistake, other coaches will remember how that athlete treated them.

Also, when a recruit makes a call to a coach to let them know they are going elsewhere, some coaches might still work to get the recruit to change their mind. While the percentage of coaches that don't honor verbal scholarship offers is relatively low, the percentage of kids who change their minds is much greater. And some of the best recruiters just don't give up easily. Their persistence often overcomes resistance.

In fact, I recently recruited a few athletes from a school where the head coach was a personal friend. I reached out to him about two guys on his roster I wanted, and he told me they weren't interested. Instead of giving up, I reached out to their club coach and received a call from the recruits, and two days later they visited campus. Four days after their campus visit, they committed to accepting the scholarship offers, much to the dismay of several Division I universities, not only in Missouri, but the surrounding states as well. It was a good thing I didn't give up after their high school coach told me they weren't interested.

16. WHEN CAN COLLEGE COACHES BEGIN THE FORMAL RECRUITING PROCESS AND MEET WITH/TALK TO RECRUITS?

Coaches are prohibited from meeting with recruits until July 1 following the student's junior year of high school. Email conversations prior to that date are allowed.

The student is also prohibited from recruiting campus visits until September 1 of their senior year of high school.

17. What role do parents play in scholarship negotiations, and what are some of their biggest mistakes?

Parents definitely need to be involved in the financial discussions related to where their son or daughter goes to school. Why? Because it's not usually the student who is the one paying for their education. Most kids don't have a firm grasp on costs, loans, and interest.

However, the tone of the personal interactions between the coach, the athlete, and the athlete's parents has a lot to do with how coaches will handle a recruit. Most coaches are trying to figure out what a parent can pay and what they want to pay. When the coach makes an offer within the range of what a parent can pay and what they want to pay (which can be two different things), they pretty much expect a recruit to accept it.

If a parent wants to pay $X, and with the help of scholarships a coach knows the best he or she can do is to get costs down to $2X, it's not a matter of whether or not they like the recruit. It is more a matter of whether or not they have enough scholarship dollars available to make it a win-win deal. If the coach doesn't have the money available, it doesn't mean they don't like the athlete; it just means they won't be recruiting them.

Everybody has needs and wants. And if the recruit, their parents, and the institution can all get their needs and wants met, it's a pretty easy, win-win process.

One of the biggest mistakes parents make is that they outspend their budget. They fall in love with the idea of their kid going to a prestigious school that, when all is said and done, even with the help of partial scholarships, is out of their price range. They maximize what they can take out in loans and may not be able to scale down the costs of their lifestyle accordingly. Or something bad happens like a job loss or a health issue that requires an extended leave and drains whatever is left in savings, and their kid can't finish school. I encourage parents to make sure they leave some financial cushion in place and give themselves financial leeway to handle unforeseen or unexpected expenses.

A second mistake parents make is walking in to meetings with coaches bragging about how great and wonderful their kid is. Every parent thinks their kid is great and wonderful. And the coaches realize that every athlete is their parent's pride and joy. Sure, your child is special, to you, and they should be. It's helpful to remember that every other child is special to their parents as well, and it doesn't sway coaches or impress them more because you say wonderful things about your child.

Another big mistake parents make is overvaluing what their kid is worth to a program. Based on performance standards that have been achieved by an athlete, coaches know what kind of contribution they can expect from an athlete. And most offer accordingly.

To a parent, potential means additional value to a program. To a coach, potential means the athlete hasn't done it yet.

Nine out of 10 parents are totally off base and clueless about the real value their child could bring to a program. Why? It's because most parents haven't taken the time to do their research or homework to find out what the wants and needs are of the college program their child is interested in competing for.

For example, if a coach gets a letter from a girl who is jumping 16 feet in the long jump, along with a letter saying she thinks she can contribute to the team, when it takes jumps of over 20 feet to score points at the conference track meet, it's obvious that neither the athlete nor her parents did their homework. If a girl is the seventh runner on an average high school cross country program and is expecting consideration from a Division I cross country coach, it isn't realistic and is a waste of time to bother the coach at that program.

For a bigger, more established Division I program, a high school boy who runs a 4:14 mile might earn a walk-on slot or something like a $2,000-per-year scholarship, especially if the current roster is loaded with plenty of guys who can run that fast or faster. For a smaller Division I program, that kind of time from the exact same boy might generate an offer to cover tuition or a little more. To the right Division II program, if the coach sees an upside in the kid and some other intangibles, that same athlete might be worth as much as 75% to a full scholarship offer. It's all a matter of matching the needs and wants of the athletes with the needs and wants of the coach.

The needs and wants of coaches vary from program to program, and what they are willing to offer in scholarship money varies also, depending on those needs and wants. The same athlete might be worth significantly more to one coach than another based on the makeup of the existing roster.

That is why it is so important for parents and athletes to do their homework, pick multiple programs where it is possible to make an impact, and reach out to them. The 10-10-10 plan gets athletes reaching out to more than just a few coaches. It creates additional options and more choices. The more choices an athlete has and the better those choices are, the less that athlete is likely to pay for college and the better the chances are that the athlete will end up somewhere they like and want to be.

If a coach throws out a lowball offer initially, the recruit simply doesn't have to accept it. This is a business deal, and it helps to have a firm grasp on the real value that an athlete can bring to the table without being unreasonable. The appropriate way to counter lowball offers is to have the athlete and their parents do their homework so they have a realistic idea of their true value and the athlete's ability to contribute to a particular college's roster. The other way to counter lowball offers is to cast a wide enough net that the recruit gets numerous other offers to choose from; then they can simply thank the coach who made the lowball offer, but let them know that the recruit has already received offers that are significantly higher and have to be considered first. If the coach really wants the recruit and has the scholarship funds available, the recruit may get another, much better offer.

18. What Questions Should Recruits Ask of Potential Teammates, and What Should They Look For From the Coach During Recruiting Visits?

A lot of coaches, during the recruiting process, may be able to make it look like their program is without morale problems. Unfortunately, the truth might not be revealed until after a recruit signs on the dotted line to accept a scholarship. After that, it's too late. That's why it is important to ask potential teammates the following questions.

1.   What is the coach like outside of practice?

2. How is the coach about missing practice for academic-related activities or endeavors?

3. How does the coach react to requests to miss practice to participate in events outside of the university, like weddings, family vacations, or any other special family obligations?

4. What is the morale of the team?

5. How well do professors work with athletes who have to miss class and/or tests to attend athletic competitions?

6. What do they like most about the university and the athletic program?

7. What do they like least about the university and the athletic program?

It is also important for a recruit to listen and observe how the current athletes talk about their coach. Do they make jokes, and if so, are the jokes made in a respectful way? Or are the jokes demeaning and indicative of a lack of respect?

Are the current athletes comfortable coming up to their coach or acknowledging their coach in public places like the cafeteria? Or does the coach have to summon or call the athletes over to talk? If a coach has to summon an athlete in public places and the athlete doesn't take some initiative to say hello or seem glad to see the coach, there might not be a good relationship there.

Now, if a current athlete is a sprinter and the coach in question is the distance coach or a field events coach, that's a different story. If a coach who doesn't coach that athlete doesn't come over, it's not necessarily a negative. However, if that coach does come over and shows interest in current athletes that are not their responsibility, then that is definitely a plus and shows that the culture of that program is a healthy one where coaches are engaged and invested in their team and the athletes that comprise it.

There are some coaches who are what I refer to as "3-5 coaches," and that's because when practice isn't taking place, they aren't heavily invested in what their athletes are doing. I make a special point, each week, to stop by and watch and visit with sprinters, throwers, jumpers, vaulters, and distance runners, even though I don't coach all of them. I pay attention to how they are doing as much if not more than I pay attention to what they are doing. If something seems off, I will call them or text them later that evening to ask how things are going. I'm invested in their well-being off of the athletic fields as much as I am on them, and I think most of the best coaches are, too.

When a recruit is visiting a campus, they have the opportunity to observe current athletes and coaches. It is important to look for subtle signs that something isn't right, or that it is.

19. WHAT'S THE DEAL WITH REDSHIRTING?

Because athletes improve as they get older, some schools will "redshirt" an athlete so they can have them competing for their school after five years of development. The catch is that one of those years, they cannot officially compete for the school. Sometimes a school will have an athlete redshirt (sit out) a year because they want to develop them and use them later. Sometimes an injury will set an athlete back and a coach might opt to redshirt the athlete instead of having them perform poorly or not at all while injured or recovering from injury.

In high school kids often play two or three sports. In college they usually focus on one.

In college cross country/track and field, athletes can expect to be training six or seven days a week for nine months. It is also likely that at some point in time, injuries are likely to occur, and the kids will come back stronger. Coaches understand periodization and microcycles and have systems in place to minimize injury risks and maximize performance.

The university owes any scholarship money promised even during the time an athlete is redshirting and not performing. So that means an athlete can get up to five years of college paid for even though they can only compete officially for four of those years, regardless of whether or not an athlete was redshirted and held out of completion for injury or for developmental purposes.

Some of the smaller schools aren't as likely to redshirt athletes for developmental purposes, because they don't want to tie up a year's worth of scholarship money in an athlete who can't be scoring points for them in competitions. Different schools have different feelings and policies about redshirting, and this varies based on the size, funding, and culture of each program.

20. WHAT DO PARENTS AND RECRUITS NEED TO KNOW ABOUT A HOME VISIT BY A COACH?

When a coach comes to visit a recruit at home, he or she will have a game plan and an idea of what they think the athlete is worth to the school. The coach is there to observe the family dynamic and get an idea of what they think the family can afford. The coach is looking to get a feel for the financial stability of the family.

The goal of the parents is to take the coach off their game. One way to do this is to have a big home-cooked meal. Once the coach has been fed and they get comfortable, they become much more relaxed.

The parents and the recruit should also have a list of questions. And Ideally, each question should load into another question.

21. WHAT ABOUT SUMMER SCHOOL?

One thing parents and recruits should ask about, but many don't realize they should, is summer school. If an athlete is offered a partial scholarship, it is a good idea to inquire as to whether summer school is included.

Summer school is an option for good students as well as those who struggle. Good students can finish their degree early and make progress toward an additional major or a graduate degree. Academically challenged athletes might want to take classes in the summer so they can carry a lighter load during the season and still graduate on time.

It can be a great opportunity for an athlete to stay on campus and train, get a part time job and work experience, and advance their education. It is a mistake not to ask about summer school or take advantage of the additional opportunities it offers.

22. What are "official" and "unofficial visits," and what do recruits need to know?

There are two types of college recruiting visits. One type is known as an "official visit," and the other is known as an "unofficial visit."

An official visit is one where the university will invite a recruit onto campus and cover the costs of meals, lodging, activities, and sometimes gas money or airline tickets for the recruit while they are on campus

An unofficial visit is one where a recruit visits a campus and every expense is covered by the recruit and/or their parents. The school can't buy so much as a candy bar for the recruit without changing the definition of that visit.

A recruit is allowed a total of only five official visits to Division I schools, and it is important to use them wisely. Once the five official visits have been used up, a recruit is allowed to visit additional universities, but it must be done at their own expense. There are no limits to the number of official visits an athlete is allowed to take at the Division II, Division III, or NAIA level.

Some hyper-competitive coaches play games with recruits. One of their games is to keep recruits on the phone for a long time without talking about money. Coaches know that if they have one recruit tied up in a long phone conversation, then other coaches (their rivals) can't get through.

Another game coaches play is when they invite an athlete on an official visit but have no plans to offer any serious scholarship money. Why would they do this? It's simple. It forces an athlete to burn one of their official visits, and might keep them from visiting an additional rival.

Think about it. An inner-city kid with limited income might not be able to afford any unofficial visits at all. And even if that athlete gets a full scholarship offer, if it comes from a school they've never visited, it is highly likely (almost certain) that they won't go there if they haven't seen the school.

23. IF A RECRUIT ISN'T SURE WHAT DIVISION A COLLEGE OR UNIVERSITY IS IN, HOW CAN THEY FIND OUT?

As of the date of this publishing, the following link at the NCAA site should allow you to find this and other information quickly and easily:

http://www.ncaa.org/about/who-we-are/search-school.

24. WHAT IS THE NATIONAL LETTER OF INTENT (NLI)?

The NLI is an agreement signed by the college-bound athlete in which they commit to attending a specific college or university for one academic year in exchange for a commitment from that university to provide financial aid for one year. This agreement is administered by the NCAA.

25. WHAT IS A "DEAD PERIOD"?

It is a period of time when a college coach may not have any in-person contact with an athlete or the athlete's parents, either on campus or off. However, coaches may write, email, or talk with an athlete or the athlete's parents via telephone during this period.

26. WHAT IS AN NCAA ID NUMBER, AND WHY IS IT IMPORTANT?

Any time a student or parent calls the NCAA Eligibility Center with questions, the NCAA ID number along with the proper password will be necessary to receive assistance. It is also the number that coaches and people on their college's compliance staff use to request certification.

27. WHAT IS THE IDEAL TIMELINE FOR ATHLETE MARKETING OUTREACH?

By April or May of a student-athlete's junior year in high school, the process should be well under way. Kids should have narrowed their list of choices, reached out to college coaches, and sent their portfolios (see the 10-10-10 plan).

If a kid goes to an academically sound school and has performed well athletically, then they might already be on the radar of some college coaches who are savvy enough to engage in conversations early on and begin developing relationships with kids they may eventually want to recruit.

CONCLUSION

So there you have it. You now know how the college recruiting game works for parents, athletes, and coaches. There should be few, if any, surprises now that you know the most common mistakes and how to avoid them.

It is my sincere wish that every athlete will find the best environment to learn, grow, and compete. I wish that as many student-athletes as possible could avoid unnecessary amounts of student debt in order to obtain their college degrees. And I hope that the additional guidance and preparation I have suggested in these pages is enough to streamline the recruiting process for coaches who have been unnecessarily tied up communicating with parents and athletes who haven't done their homework and aren't ideally suited for their programs.

My goal in writing this book was to create a win-win-win situation for parents, athletes, and coaches.

SPECIAL INVITATION: Contact information appears below that could be helpful if you or anyone you know needs special coaching beyond what's written in these pages. If you or someone you know wants confidential feedback on any of the following items, you can use my contact information provided below:

-**scholarship offers**

-**portfolio design**

-**individual/private athletic coaching**

Coach Vince Bingham

Email: RunJumpThrowBook@gmail.com

www.CoachVinceBingham.com

ABOUT THE AUTHOR

Coach Vince Bingham

Vince Bingham returned to Lindenwood University in 2016 after spending three seasons as assistant track coach at Northern Illinois University. Bingham's athletes broke 16 school records in three years, and qualified for the NCAA Regional Championships in six events.

Prior to Northern Illinois, Bingham served as head coach at Neosho County Community College (NCCC) in Chanute, Kansas. As the head coach at NCCC in 2012-13, Bingham led the Panthers to a stellar season in both indoor and outdoor competition. NCCC brought home seven All-Americans from the NJCAA national meet in March, and followed that up with 11 individual All-Americans at the outdoor national championships. As a team, Bingham's Panthers placed ninth on the women's side and eighth in the final men's standings.

Prior to working at NCCC, Bingham spent time as a head coach at Missouri Baptist, and as an assistant coach at Kansas University, Southern Illinois University, University of Missouri, Lincoln University, and Lindenwood University.

Bingham served as the Director of Track Operations at Kansas from 2009 to 2011. During his two years in Lawrence, he not only helped with the day-to-day operations, but also assisted in helping the Jayhawks place in the top 25 at the NCAA Outdoor Championships. His recruiting efforts also lifted the once-unranked Kansas to the 2013 NCAA national outdoor title.

Bingham also found plenty of success as the head coach at Missouri Baptist. In 2006, he led the Spartans to NAIA national titles at both the indoor and outdoor meets that year. His team also set eight NAIA national records at the 2006 indoor meet and saw 18 of its 21 athletes earn All-American status. At the 2006 outdoor meet, Missouri Baptist took home eight individual titles. In total, Bingham's athletes brought home 78 All-American honors on both the men's and women's sides to help him net the NAIA National Track & Field Coach of the Year Award in 2006. Off the track, Missouri Baptist had five NAIA scholar-athletes.

In 1998, Bingham was an assistant on Lindenwood's men's indoor national championship squad, which won the school's first national championship.

All told, Bingham has helped coach 14 different athletes to NAIA championships. Additionally, he has coached seven Olympians: Nickeisha Anderson (Jamaica, 2008), Ibrahim Bashir (Kuwait, 2004), Brittany Borman (United States, 2012 & 2016), Nikki Holder (Canada, 2012 & 2012), Randy Lewis (Grenada, 2004 & 2008), Lanece Clark (Bahamas, 2016; 4x400), and John Ampoham (Ghana, 2016; javelin).

Bingham currently serves the Ozark Youth Association as USATF Executive Board Member, USATF Youth Vice Chair, and AAU Youth Chair. Bingham was inducted into the Missouri High

School Cross Country/Track Coaches Hall of Fame in 2015.

ACKNOWLEDGMENTS

I want to thank every parent, coach, teammate, and business owner who has ever supported me, my teammates, and the young athletes I've gotten opportunities to work with. I'm especially thankful for the contributors behind the scenes who donate their time, expertise, and financial resources to make dreams a reality for kids facing limited opportunities or obstacles that might otherwise hold them back.

By no means is this list exhaustive, but I want the following people to know that I especially appreciate them and am truly thankful they have been part of my life:

Lillie Mae Bingham

James Bingham

Denise Bingham

William Bingham

Harriett and Deotis Block

The Jennings Family

The Cook Family

The Borman Family

Scott Roberts

Connie Teaberry

Clark Willie

Tom Smith

Rick McQuire

Stanley Redwine

Tom Doyle

Heather Gilbert

Eddie Harris

Coach Vince Bingham

Email: <u>RunJumpThrowBook@gmail.com</u>

www.CoachVinceBingham.com

www.ingramcontent.com/pod-product-compliance
Lightning Source LLC
LaVergne TN
LVHW021501080426
835509LV00018B/2359